CHILD OF GOD

46 Biblical Affirmations for Kids

BY VIVIANN FLOYD

warnerpress.org

© 2024 Warner Press, Inc.   Printed in USA   All rights reserved
305800215287

I AM BRAVE

Read 1 Samuel 17:20-49

It's not always easy being brave in times of trouble. Fear and doubt try to creep in, and it can be difficult to stay confident. David was a young boy who displayed a grown man's bravery in a fearful situation. He stood up against Goliath, the giant Philistine soldier, and defeated him with God's help using only a stone and a sling. David is a great example that I can be brave and stand up for what is right, no matter my size.

THE SPIRIT GOD GAVE US DOES NOT MAKE US TIMID, BUT GIVES US POWER, LOVE AND SELF-DISCIPLINE.

—2 Timothy 1:7

I AM KIND

Read Acts 9:26–30

Kindness is a gift that should never be taken for granted. It is no small thing to be able to encourage someone else. Barnabas encouraged the apostles to accept Paul after he accepted Jesus as his Savior. He also mentored the young John Mark when no one else wanted to give him a second chance. God uses people to uplift and help other people. I never know what someone else is going through. Kindness is a simple way of showing love to another person.

**BE KIND AND COMPASSIONATE TO ONE ANOTHER,
FORGIVING EACH OTHER,
JUST AS IN CHRIST GOD FORGAVE YOU.**

—Ephesians 4:32

I AM IMPORTANT

Everything about me is important. Even before the universe was created, God had me in mind. He made me very special, and my life has a purpose. It is only in God that I can discover my purpose and my identity. The Lord Jesus cares about everything that concerns me. If it matters to me, then it matters to Him. I am so important that God wants me to rely on Him for all that I need.

WE ARE GOD'S HANDIWORK, CREATED IN CHRIST JESUS TO DO GOOD WORKS, WHICH GOD PREPARED IN ADVANCE FOR US TO DO.

—Ephesians 2:10

I AM A GOOD LEADER

Read 2 Kings 22:1-7

Before I can be a leader to others, I have to know how to serve others. Jesus was the prime example of a leader, but He humbled Himself to serve His disciples by washing their feet (a servant's task) during the Last Supper. Another biblical example of a great leader was Josiah. He began his reign as king at 8 years old and became one of the greatest rulers of Israel. Second Kings 22:2 says, "He did what was right in the eyes of the LORD." The most effective way to lead others is by being a good example.

DON'T LET ANYONE LOOK DOWN ON YOU BECAUSE YOU ARE YOUNG, BUT SET AN EXAMPLE FOR THE BELIEVERS IN SPEECH, IN CONDUCT, IN LOVE, IN FAITH AND IN PURITY.
—1 Timothy 4:12

I AM SMART

Read 1 Kings 3:5-13

I can use wisdom in making good choices. Solomon, a king of Israel, was a great example of asking God for wisdom. Everything that I do first begins in the mind. It's very important to feed my mind with thoughts that are positive and uplifting. Asking God for wisdom, studying the Bible, and being open-minded to different points of view are qualities of an intelligent person.

THE HEART OF THE DISCERNING ACQUIRES KNOWLEDGE, FOR THE EARS OF THE WISE SEEK IT OUT.

—Proverbs 18:15

I AM LOVED

Read 1 Corinthians 13:4-7, 13

The greatest gift that God has given to me is love. It's more powerful than any other feeling or emotion there is. Every living thing that's been created desires love. Love is like a big tree with a lot of emotions and actions branching out from it—actions such as kindness, patience, gratitude, thoughtfulness, happiness, peace, positivity, etc. The most powerful example of love was God sending His Son to teach the world of His ways and give His life on the cross for me.

FOR GOD SO LOVED THE WORLD THAT HE GAVE HIS ONE AND ONLY SON, THAT WHOEVER BELIEVES IN HIM SHALL NOT PERISH BUT HAVE ETERNAL LIFE.

—John 3:16

I AM COURAGEOUS

Read Esther 4:11–16

Courage happens when someone is facing a scary situation but chooses to do what is right anyway. Esther stood against a king and an empire to save her people from destruction. It takes courage to stand up for what is right. God is with me in every situation that comes my way. Esther is a great example of choosing courage over fear in an intimidating situation.

BE STRONG AND COURAGEOUS. DO NOT BE AFRAID; DO NOT BE DISCOURAGED, FOR THE LORD YOUR GOD WILL BE WITH YOU WHEREVER YOU GO.
—Joshua 1:9

I AM UNIQUE

Read Romans 12:4-8

No one else on earth is exactly like me. Down to the very atoms and molecules of my DNA, I was created very distinctly by God. Each one of my personal experiences are exclusive from anyone else. My individual purpose, identity, inborn characteristics, and genuine devotion to Christ are all unique.

I PRAISE YOU BECAUSE I AM FEARFULLY AND WONDERFULLY MADE.

—Psalm 139:14

I AM A LIGHT

Read Matthew 5:14-16

Sometimes the only light some people will ever see is the one in followers of Christ. I should always let my light shine so others can see Jesus through me. Jesus and the disciples were well known by multitudes of people. One reason they stood apart from everyone else was because of the distinctive light that shone through them. My light can be contagious and uplifting to others, even if I don't always realize it.

WHEN JESUS SPOKE AGAIN TO THE PEOPLE, HE SAID, "I AM THE LIGHT OF THE WORLD. WHOEVER FOLLOWS ME WILL NEVER WALK IN DARKNESS, BUT WILL HAVE THE LIGHT OF LIFE."

—John 8:12

I AM A GREAT FRIEND

Read John 15:13–15

Being a great friend is a gift; having a great friend is a blessing. Treating others the way I want to be treated is the key to both. The disciple John was an amazingly loyal friend to Jesus. He was the only one of the twelve disciples who stayed close to Jesus throughout the trial and crucifixion. John was a true friend from the beginning of Jesus' ministry until after Jesus' resurrection.

DO TO OTHERS AS YOU WOULD HAVE THEM DO TO YOU.

—Luke 6:31

I AM CREATED FOR A PURPOSE

God has an important plan for my life. I was created for a purpose. When I learn what my purpose is, then I will know my true identity in Christ. I can understand more about my spiritual identity and the purpose God has for me by studying God's Word and praying.

"FOR I KNOW THE PLANS I HAVE FOR YOU," DECLARES THE LORD, "PLANS TO PROSPER YOU AND NOT TO HARM YOU, PLANS TO GIVE YOU HOPE AND A FUTURE."

—Jeremiah 29:11

I AM NOT ALONE

Read Mark 1:35–39

At times I may feel alone, even surrounded by a crowd of people. Once I choose to accept Jesus and live by His Word, I am never alone. I may sometimes feel like I need reassurance from God that He is still with me. I can remember God is always with me by praying and reading His Word.

THE LORD HIMSELF GOES BEFORE YOU AND WILL BE WITH YOU; HE WILL NEVER LEAVE YOU NOR FORSAKE YOU.

—Deuteronomy 31:8

I AM A STUDENT

Read John 14:26-28

I always have something to learn or improve on. If I ever get to the point where I think that I know everything, then growth stops. The disciples remained students even after Jesus ascended to heaven because He sent the Advocate to them. The Holy Spirit gives direction as well as correction. My walk in life and with God is full of learning experiences. The older I get, the more I have to learn. Take one step, one task, and one day at a time.

ALL SCRIPTURE IS GOD-BREATHED AND IS USEFUL FOR TEACHING, REBUKING, CORRECTING AND TRAINING IN RIGHTEOUSNESS, SO THAT THE SERVANT OF GOD MAY BE THOROUGHLY EQUIPPED FOR EVERY GOOD WORK.

—2 Timothy 3:16-17

I AM HELPED IN TROUBLE

Read Matthew 14:28-31

Knowing that I have a helping hand in times of trouble is such a comfort. All it takes is a call out to Jesus, and He is right there to rescue me. Jesus called Peter out of the boat to walk toward Him on the sea. The moment that Peter took his eyes off Jesus and became fearful, he began to sink. He called out for the Lord to save him. Immediately, Jesus reached out His hand and rescued Peter. I will always keep my eyes on Jesus and believe that He will be there to help me whenever I need Him.

WHERE DOES MY HELP COME FROM? MY HELP COMES FROM THE LORD.

—Psalm 121:1-2

I WALK WITH INTEGRITY

Read Daniel 6:3–5

Integrity is one of the most important characteristics a person can possess. Integrity means knowing what is right and wrong and choosing to do what is right, especially when no one else is watching. Daniel was a man who had an abundance of integrity. He constantly made the decision to be honest and obey God first in all that he did. God blessed Daniel because of that.

WHOEVER WALKS IN INTEGRITY WALKS SECURELY.

—Proverbs 10:9

I AM PATIENT

Read Job 2:3-10

If you pray for patience, God will give you plenty of opportunities to learn it. Patience is a valuable and rare trait to acquire. It can be challenging to have patience in my relationships with other people, as well as with myself. Patience is a gift, and it shows love. Job had a lot of patience. He trusted God and never wavered during his struggles. Because Job had patience and was faithful to God, God blessed Job.

BE PATIENT, BEARING WITH ONE ANOTHER IN LOVE.

—Ephesians 4:2

I HAVE SELF-CONTROL

Read Nehemiah 4:11-23

Self-control comes with strength and wisdom. While Nehemiah and his men were rebuilding the walls of Jerusalem, nearby armies came to attack them. He showed self-control by not fighting back and remaining calm. Nehemiah used wisdom by posting some of his men to stand guard while the others continued to work. He was a strong man who trusted God to protect him.

LIKE A CITY WHOSE WALLS ARE BROKEN THROUGH IS A PERSON WHO LACKS SELF-CONTROL.

—Proverbs 25:28

I AM PROTECTED

Read Daniel 3:13-25

It is comforting to know that God protects and covers me under His wings like a hen shelters her chicks. He walks with me through both the good times and the bad. The three young Hebrew men were protected when they were thrown in the fiery furnace by King Nebuchadnezzar for refusing to bow down to a golden image. Three went into the furnace and three walked out, but four men were seen walking in the fire. Jesus was right there with them, and they were not hurt.

**DO NOT FEAR, FOR I AM WITH YOU;
DO NOT BE DISMAYED, FOR I AM YOUR GOD.
I WILL STRENGTHEN YOU AND HELP YOU.**

—Isaiah 41:10

I AM HONEST

Lying creates stress and guilt, but telling the truth always reaults in freedom and peace of mind. Honesty shows great character. Zacchaeus was a dishonest tax collector. After meeting and spending time with Jesus, Zacchaeus had a change of mind and heart. He chose to live an honest life and to treat people fairly. Choosing truth is like being released from chains. It absolutely makes one free.

A TRUTHFUL WITNESS SAVES LIVES, BUT A FALSE WITNESS IS DECEITFUL.

—Proverbs 14:25

I AM RESPONSIBLE

Read Matthew 25:14-21

God expects me to be responsible. A big part of growing up is learning to take responsibility for the choices that I make. Everything I do begins in my mind. There will be good and bad consequences for every choice I make. I am held accountable for what I decide to do or how I respond in a situation. I can't control what other people say or do; however, I can control how I react.

EACH OF US WILL GIVE AN ACCOUNT OF OURSELVES TO GOD.

—Romans 14:12

I AM A CHILD OF GOD

Read 1 John 3:1-3

Believing in something I cannot see can feel challenging at times, but that is how I become a child of God. He created me, but to be His child I must accept and believe that Jesus Christ is Lord. Jesus died on the cross for my sins and rose again on the third day. If I believe that to be true and allow His Word to live in me, then I am a child of God!

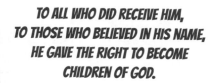

TO ALL WHO DID RECEIVE HIM, TO THOSE WHO BELIEVED IN HIS NAME, HE GAVE THE RIGHT TO BECOME CHILDREN OF GOD.

—John 1:12

I AM HAPPY

Read Isaiah 9:1-3

True happiness is a gift from the Lord. When I accept Jesus as Lord of my life, I am changed from the inside out. God mends my broken heart, helps calm my anger, and heals any wounds that I may have. When I allow God to perform spiritual surgery on me and heal any brokenness that I may have, then change will happen in my heart and mind. That is when true happiness begins.

TAKE DELIGHT IN THE LORD, AND HE WILL GIVE YOU THE DESIRES OF YOUR HEART.

—Psalm 37:4

I AM CREATIVE

Read Genesis 1

Everywhere I look, I can see how big God's imagination is. God created a beautiful place for me to live in, and He gave me the ability to share in His enjoyment. A genuine imagination opens my mind and allows me to use my God-given talents to create things like art, music, and poetry. Expressing myself in this way can help me cope with anxiety, fear, stress, and other concerns that keep me discouraged. Creativity is one of the tools that God gave me to bring both pleasure and help when needed.

WHATEVER YOU DO, WORK AT IT WITH ALL YOUR HEART, AS WORKING FOR THE LORD.
—Colossians 3:23

I AM WELCOMED

Read Mark 6:1-4

Every person wishes to feel acceptance and belonging. God knows what rejection is like, so He welcomes those who believe in Him. He forgives, restores, and gives new life to those who trust in His Son, Jesus Christ. God's love and acceptance are unconditional. He also expects me to be accepting of others in a nonjudgmental and compassionate way.

ANYONE WHO WELCOMES YOU WELCOMES ME, AND ANYONE WHO WELCOMES ME WELCOMES THE ONE WHO SENT ME.

—Matthew 10:40

I AM DETERMINED

Read 2 Timothy 4:5-8

A prime definition of determination is continuing to persevere toward a goal, no matter what sort of obstacles stand in the way. Paul stated toward the end of his life that he had "fought the good fight...finished the race...[and] kept the faith." Paul was stoned, shipwrecked three times, and imprisoned during his ministry. He never gave up and persevered to the very end. It takes a lot of strength to have that level of determination. That type of strength and motivation comes from the Lord.

LET US NOT BECOME WEARY IN DOING GOOD, FOR AT THE PROPER TIME WE WILL REAP A HARVEST IF WE DO NOT GIVE UP.

–Galatians 6:9

I AM THANKFUL

Read Colossians 3:15-17

A thankful mindset is a powerful thing. When I am grateful, I will have greater happiness and fulfillment in my life. Gratitude helps me recognize the gifts that God has given me. It also opens me up to receiving other blessings that He has in store for me. There are several benefits of thankfulness, such as reduced depression, increased feelings of happiness, lower anxiety, and improvement of energy and productivity. A positive and grateful attitude affects everything.

DO NOT BE ANXIOUS ABOUT ANYTHING, BUT IN EVERY SITUATION, BY PRAYER AND PETITION, WITH THANKSGIVING, PRESENT YOUR REQUESTS TO GOD.
—Philippians 4:6

I AM RESPECTFUL

God calls me to love and respect others. It's not always a simple thing to show respect for others, especially those who have not been kind to me. Looking past the surface and seeing the value in others doesn't mean that I must agree with their behavior. It means that I can show them love and respect because God loves them too.

DO NOT SEEK REVENGE OR BEAR A GRUDGE AGAINST ANYONE AMONG YOUR PEOPLE, BUT LOVE YOUR NEIGHBOR AS YOURSELF.

—Leviticus 19:18

WHEN I AM WEAK, JESUS IS STRONG

Read Judges 7:16-21

During my spiritual growth, I may feel I'm not where I should be in my relationship with the Lord. I might assume that because of my mistakes God can't use me. God used Gideon and helped him in his weakness of unbelief that he could save Israel. God's patient guidance assisted Gideon in defeating the Midianite army of 32,000 men with only 300 men. Everyone has faults and shortcomings. God doesn't love anyone more for being better; He just loves everyone.

HE SAID TO ME, "MY GRACE IS SUFFICIENT FOR YOU, FOR MY POWER IS MADE PERFECT IN WEAKNESS." THEREFORE I WILL BOAST ALL THE MORE GLADLY ABOUT MY WEAKNESSES, SO THAT CHRIST'S POWER MAY REST ON ME.

—2 Corinthians 12:9

I BELIEVE IN MYSELF

Read 1 Samuel 30:3-6

David said in the Book of Samuel that he strengthened himself in the Lord. There will be times when I will have to encourage myself rather than relying on others to lift me up. It is essential to stand firm on the Word of God. I believe that through Jesus, I can accomplish anything that I set my mind to.

I CAN DO ALL THIS THROUGH HIM WHO GIVES ME STRENGTH.

—Philippians 4:13

I AM A BLESSING

Read Proverbs 11:24-27

Jesus living in my heart is like having a bright light shining through me. A sincere smile and encouraging words are blessings to so many people. I am so important to God. He desires to bless me in ways that are mind-blowing. He also uses people to be blessings to other people. When I bless others, God will reward me.

LET YOUR LIGHT SHINE BEFORE OTHERS, THAT THEY MAY SEE YOUR GOOD DEEDS AND GLORIFY YOUR FATHER IN HEAVEN.

—Matthew 5:16

I AM NOTICED

Read Psalm 139:2-4

There is nothing about me that God doesn't notice. He sees the real me. Every thought in my head and every feeling in my heart is known by God. People may not always pay attention, but the Lord does. Everything that concerns me, concerns God, no matter how big or small. It matters to Him because I am His child.

INDEED, THE VERY HAIRS OF YOUR HEAD ARE ALL NUMBERED. DON'T BE AFRAID; YOU ARE WORTH MORE THAN MANY SPARROWS.

—Luke 12:7

I AM AN ENCOURAGER

Read Hebrews 10:23-25

At times, it takes a stronger effort to encourage someone rather than criticize. There are so many things in life that can tear a person down. I will follow the example of Jesus and lift others up. A heart-felt compliment or kind words can make a tremendous difference to a troubled soul. I strive to be a light and brighten someone's day.

ENCOURAGE ONE ANOTHER AND BUILD EACH OTHER UP, JUST AS IN FACT YOU ARE DOING.

—1 Thessalonians 5:11

I AM CONFIDENT

Read Exodus 5:1-4; 12:50-51

Confidence is a mindset; however, it is not boastful or arrogant. The first step is believing in my abilities and gifts that are given to me by God. The second step is taking action and doing what I am called to do. While believing that God is with me, I also must believe in myself. Moses had to have confidence when he faced Pharaoh and led his people out of bondage in Egypt. God was with him the entire time.

THOSE WHO HOPE IN THE LORD WILL RENEW THEIR STRENGTH. THEY WILL SOAR ON WINGS LIKE EAGLES; THEY WILL RUN AND NOT GROW WEARY, THEY WILL WALK AND NOT BE FAINT.

—Isaiah 40:31

I AM BRAND NEW

Read Ezekiel 11:19-20

When I chose to accept Jesus into my heart, I became spiritually born again. I am a brand-new creation in God. Becoming a Christian does not signify that all my problems will disappear. It simply means that Jesus is now walking through my struggles with me. I have a new mindset and no longer have to go through trials or tribulations alone.

THEREFORE, IF ANYONE IS IN CHRIST, THE NEW CREATION HAS COME: THE OLD HAS GONE, THE NEW IS HERE!

—2 Corinthians 5:17

I AM COMPASSIONATE

A perfect illustration for compassion is found in the Book of Luke. Two people passed by a wounded man left on the side of the road after being robbed. A Samaritan, showing compassion, stopped to help the hurt stranger and paid for his care. I never know what someone might be going through, but I will show love and compassion to help others in need.

LOVE YOUR ENEMIES, DO GOOD TO THEM, AND LEND TO THEM WITHOUT EXPECTING TO GET ANYTHING BACK. THEN YOUR REWARD WILL BE GREAT, AND YOU WILL BE CHILDREN OF THE MOST HIGH.

—Luke 6:35

I AM GENEROUS

Read 2 Kings 4:8-10

God expects me to treat others with kindness and a giving heart. The Shunammite Woman made a permanent place for Elisha to stay whenever he passed through town, because she knew he was a man of God. In many ways, the mere act of being charitable is its own reward. I will be good to others in love just as I would want in return. God loves a cheerful giver!

LET US DO GOOD TO ALL PEOPLE, ESPECIALLY TO THOSE WHO BELONG TO THE FAMILY OF BELIEVERS.

—Galatians 6:10

I AM CARED FOR

Read 1 Peter 5:6-7

It's amazing how God always knows exactly what I need even better than I do. He goes before me to make sure I am taken care of in the best possible way. Jesus makes ways when there doesn't seem to be a way. When I feel like I am at the end of the rope and my resources are slim, God always provides. I am His child, and He cares for me in every way.

MY GOD WILL MEET ALL YOUR NEEDS ACCORDING TO THE RICHES OF HIS GLORY IN CHRIST JESUS.

—Philippians 4:19

I AM FAITHFUL

Read Ruth 1:15-17

Someone who is faithful is loyal and reliable. Ruth was loyal to her mother-in-law, Naomi, and became faithful to God. Leaving her homeland after her husband died, Ruth chose to follow Naomi to Bethlehem. Through Naomi's example, Ruth learned of God and followed Him for the rest of her days. God faithfully blessed Ruth for her love as well as her unmoving loyalty.

FOR THE WORD OF THE LORD IS RIGHT AND TRUE; HE IS FAITHFUL IN ALL HE DOES.

—Psalm 33:4

I AM BOLD

Read 1 Kings 18:31-39

Elijah was a very bold prophet of God who bravely defended the Lord against false gods. During that time, idolatry was rampant; however, Elijah did not back down from proclaiming that the Lord is the only true living God. Confidence, bravery, and honesty are a few characteristics of being bold. At the same time, it is also important to be humble enough to know when to seek God for guidance, as well as wisdom.

LET US THEN APPROACH GOD'S THRONE OF GRACE WITH CONFIDENCE, SO THAT WE MAY RECEIVE MERCY AND FIND GRACE TO HELP US IN OUR TIME OF NEED.

—Hebrews 4:16

I AM A HARD WORKER

Read Acts 9:28-41

Anything that is worth having or doing takes hard work. When things are worked for, they are appreciated more. God rewards diligent hard work, which builds character and leadership qualities. Peter and Paul (also known as Saul) were two of the hardest working and dedicated people in the Bible. They were dedicated leaders who stayed the course to the very end. I will strive to follow their example.

**WHATEVER YOU DO,
WORK AT IT WITH ALL YOUR HEART,
AS WORKING FOR THE LORD,
NOT FOR HUMAN MASTERS.**

—Colossians 3:23

I AM THOUGHTFUL

Read Joshua 2:2-21

Being thoughtful means having consideration of others and giving attention to their needs ahead of our own. Rahab was a thoughtful woman that chose to put herself at risk by hiding the spies that Joshua sent to scout Jericho. As a result of her attentive and kind heart, God saved her and her family when the walls of Jericho were destroyed. Sincere thoughtfulness is always rewarded.

DO NOTHING OUT OF SELFISH AMBITION OR VAIN CONCEIT. RATHER, IN HUMILITY VALUE OTHERS ABOVE YOURSELVES, NOT LOOKING TO YOUR OWN INTERESTS BUT EACH OF YOU TO THE INTERESTS OF THE OTHERS.

—Philippians 2:3-4

I AM HUMBLE

Read Daniel 4:29-34

Learning to become humble is not easy, but it is very gratifying. It is the opposite of walking in pride. Because of his pride, King Nebuchadnezzar was made to live away from his kingdom as a wild animal and was unable to speak. After seven years, he came to know that God was the one in control of everything. He was then allowed to return to his kingdom with a new mindset.

NOW I, NEBUCHADNEZZAR, PRAISE AND EXALT AND GLORIFY THE KING OF HEAVEN, BECAUSE EVERYTHING HE DOES IS RIGHT AND ALL HIS WAYS ARE JUST. AND THOSE WHO WALK IN PRIDE HE IS ABLE TO HUMBLE.

—Daniel 4:37

I AM COMFORTED

Comfort is comparable to a valuable treasure. After the resurrection, Jesus fellowshipped with the disciples for forty days. During that time, He continued to instruct them on what they would need to know in order to continue to spread the gospel. He also said that He would send the Advocate, which is the Holy Spirit, to help them. God's Spirit living inside of me is my lifeline. There is no help or comfort greater than the Holy Spirit.

COME TO ME, ALL YOU WHO ARE WEARY AND BURDENED, AND I WILL GIVE YOU REST.

—Matthew 11:28

45

I AM STRONG

Read Judges 16:4-19, 28

When thinking of a strong person in the Bible, Samson is usually one of the first that comes to mind. His fearsome strength was a gift from God. When Samson chose to take his eyes off God, he became deceived, which resulted in losing his strength. In the end, God showed mercy and allowed Samson to use his strength one last time. The choices that I make affect my life and can have serious consequences. It takes a strong person to pause, use wisdom, and seek God before making big decisions.

BUT YOU, LORD, DO NOT BE FAR FROM ME. YOU ARE MY STRENGTH.

—Psalm 22:19

I AM CALM DURING A STORM

Read Mark 4:35-41

Who sleeps peacefully out on the sea, in the middle of a massive storm? Only the Lord. The panicked disciples woke Jesus in fear of being destroyed by the storm. He immediately calmed the winds and told the waves to be still. He then asked the disciples, "Where is your faith?" It can be difficult to hear Jesus when a storm is raging around me. Faith is an anchor to hold onto until the storm passes; knowing that the Master of the sea is with me.

WHEN YOU PASS THROUGH THE WATERS, I WILL BE WITH YOU; AND WHEN YOU PASS THROUGH THE RIVERS, THEY WILL NOT SWEEP OVER YOU. WHEN YOU WALK THROUGH THE FIRE, YOU WILL NOT BE BURNED.

—Isaiah 43:2

I CAN TRUST GOD

Read Romans 4:18-24

Sometimes it can be hard to trust other people, but God can always be trusted. He is our Father and wants us to know that He has our best interests at heart, without fail. Especially since He can see further down the road than we can. Every single person in the Bible that was used by God had to first learn to trust Him. None of those people were ever let down or forgotten by God, and I will not be either.

TRUST IN THE LORD WITH ALL YOUR HEART AND LEAN NOT ON YOUR OWN UNDERSTANDING; IN ALL YOUR WAYS SUBMIT TO HIM, AND HE WILL MAKE YOUR PATHS STRAIGHT.

—Proverbs 3:5-6